LAUNCEST
CASTLE

CORNWALL

❖

A D Saunders

Launceston Castle dates from the early years of the Norman Conquest. Towering over the town, it is a reminder of the power of the Earls (later Dukes) of Cornwall. Built by William the Conqueror's half-brother, Count Robert of Mortain, the castle was extensively remodelled by Richard, Earl of Cornwall, in the mid-thirteenth century. After his death, the centre of the earldom's administration moved, the castle's importance declined, and it became a prison and the site of the county jail.

Little survives of the castle now other than its defences: the mound with its stone keep and High Tower, the ruined gatehouses and curtain wall, together with the impressive earthworks. Excavation has revealed more evidence, including the Great Hall.

This guidebook gives visitors a tour and description of the castle, and a summary of its history and those connected with it.

❖ CONTENTS ❖

Visit our website at www.english-heritage.org.uk
Published by English Heritage,
1 Waterhouse Square, 138-142 Holborn, London EC1N 2ST
Copyright © English Heritage 1998
FIRST PUBLISHED 1998
Revised edition 2002
Reprinted 2005, 2007, 2009, 2011, 2013
Photographs by English Heritage Photographic Unit and
copyright of English Heritage, unless otherwise stated.
Edited by Lorimer Poultney
Designed by Grahame Dudley Associates
Printed in England by The Colourhouse
ISBN 978-1-85074-020-9
05/13 C25 03562

WORLD
LAND
TRUST™

www.carbonbalancedpaper.com
CBP00037792904130437

INTRODUCTION

❖

LAUNCESTON CASTLE dates back to the Norman Conquest. Towering over the roofs of the town it was, and still is, a reminder of the authority of the Earls (later Dukes) of Cornwall. Yet very little of the castle survives other than its defences: the mound (or 'motte') with its stone keep, the ruined gatehouses and some lengths of stone curtain wall. The most obvious features are the earthworks, and the high mound, half natural and half artificial, which formed the citadel of a rectangular embanked courtyard (or 'bailey') built on a steeply sloping ridge.

The site was highly defensible, in terms of eleventh-century warfare,

but must have been both inconvenient and restricted for all the buildings that were essential for the principal castle of one of the leading barons of medieval England. A medieval castle had several roles. It was not just a fortress, first established to dominate a hostile population and later prove the lord's military power, but also a 'country house' to which its lord might go in the course of a grand progress after many years' absence and entertain on a lavish scale. It was also an administrative centre for vast estates, where rents were paid, courts were held, judgements given and punishment exacted. Although the local people might never see the earl

View of the keep and the approach to the mound

himself, his presence and authority were ever dominant in their lives. This presence belonged to the castle, the symbol of feudal power and the status of its owner.

In recent years, archaeology has added to what is known about the castle from historical sources. Excavation has revealed the sequence and character of the defences and the sort of buildings that occupied the courtyard throughout the Middle Ages. The original defences were principally of wood backed with clay and rubble ramparts, and the interior was packed with temporary huts of the initial garrison as well as a timber great hall.

These wooden structures were replaced by more substantial stone-based buildings; the defences were reconstructed, though still with timber breastworks. The masonry keep on the mound appears to belong to the late twelfth century, but it is not known what it replaced.

The greatest changes came in the thirteenth century when Richard of Cornwall, younger brother of King Henry III, was earl. The defences were remodelled with the insertion of the High Tower within the keep, the reconstruction of the gatehouses and the building of a continuous stone curtain wall around the courtyard. Most of the stone walls you can see today date from this time. Within the

bailey, there was major rebuilding (including the Great Hall and the kitchen) and a radical rearrangement of the buildings.

A further significant change occurred towards the end of the thirteenth century when Richard's son, Edmund, decided to move the administrative element of the castle from Launceston to Lostwithiel. This led to a decline in the castle's importance, although its buildings were still numerous and maintained during the fourteenth and fifteenth centuries. By the advent of the Tudors, though, castles such as Launceston were redundant both militarily and residentially. By the time of a Parliamentary Survey of 1650 there were no buildings left standing in the bailey.

The castle was not wholly dead, however. Assizes (law courts) were held in the Great Hall until about 1610 and a prison kept in the North Gatehouse, the residence of the constable. The county jail was later established in the bailey and acquired notoriety for its cramped and unhygienic conditions. This was demolished in 1842 after the assizes were moved to Bodmin. The castle thus had no function left. It was then drastically 'landscaped' and turned into a public park. Since 1984 it has been in the care of English Heritage, although it remains in the ownership of the Duchy of Cornwall.

DESCRIPTION AND TOUR

❖

The castle is built mainly with the local shale stone, which can weather badly. Architectural details, such as door and window openings, are in a local volcanic stone known as Polyphant stone (the name derives from a village about 6km [4 miles] from Launceston). Granite from Bodmin Moor is sometimes used as well. The principal buildings were roofed with local slate, and crested by clay ridge-tiles.

SOUTH GATEHOUSE

This is the main entrance to the castle today. In medieval times it was the gateway to the castle park and faced

The outside of the South Gatehouse

Reconstruction drawing by Peter Dunn of the South Gatehouse in the fourteenth century, looking from the courtyard

away from the town. Erosion has caused the ground level to drop so that what visitors see today is not at the same level as in the Middle Ages: if you stand directly under the gateway arch, the original entrance level is at about your head height.

The medieval roadway continued out over a 'barbican', or fortified stone bridge, across a ditch to where the Victorian Guildhall now stands. The first pair of arches of this bridge, now blocked with masonry, can be seen just inside from the pavement. The ledge for the bridge's timber decking is above the arches and over it are two opposed cross loops (arrow slits) in arched recesses in the high walls which protect access to the bridge. The ditch and all but the inner end of the bridge were destroyed in 1834 during the construction of St Thomas's Road.

The gatehouse was built, rebuilt and extended over three centuries. The first gatehouse probably belongs to the twelfth century. The major refacing, which involved the addition of two shallow and solid drum towers to create a high and imposing entrance, is part of Richard of Cornwall's thirteenth-century rebuilding. The fortified bridge or barbican described above dates from the fourteenth century. Apart from its front wall, very little of the gatehouse survives. There is evidence for rooms on the first and second floors, lit by windows, and reached up an external stone stair on the eastern side which also gave access to the wall walk of the curtain wall.

NORTH GATEHOUSE

In the Middle Ages this gate was known as the 'Town Gate', and led directly into the town. Its significance lies in the fact that the castle's constable (the earl's senior resident official) had his apartments over the gate passage. Little remains of the gatehouse after the demolitions of 1764 other than the gate passage and the ground-floor room alongside it. Even the outer front of the gatehouse has been cut back and there is now no sign of the ditch in front or of the bridge which formerly crossed it.

The gatehouse itself was built in the second half of the thirteenth century, probably as the last stage of Richard of Cornwall's remodelling of the castle. The bailey rampart was cut back to build the present gatehouse, and from this and other features it seems likely that the original Town Gate was located elsewhere along this side of the bailey. Just inside the gate arch is the slot for the portcullis.

A pointed archway leads into a rectangular room. The constable's chamber was probably above this room, with his hall being above the gate passage. The room is lit by three narrow rectangular loops, only one of which is complete. There is a wall cupboard just inside the doorway. Originally, this room may have been used by a porter. Later it was used as a prison, as the plaque to the Quaker George Fox reminds us (see page 20).

At the far end of the room is a stone-lined pit or cellar. This is an earlier feature with a slightly different alignment incorporated into the late thirteenth-century gatehouse. The pit is thought to be the base of a stone tower, one of at least three that were added to the twelfth-century timber wall of the courtyard rampart.

The 'pit' was reused, perhaps as a prison, but later a stone arch was inserted, maybe to convert it to a latrine. The broken walling and subsequent blocking in the far wall represent a modern breach for a doorway.

THE COURTYARD OR BAILEY

The courtyard or bailey enclosed the main buildings of the castle. The area is roughly rectangular in shape, with the huge mound occupying the north-eastern corner. The earthen rampart is massively high to the east and continues round to the south, with the South Gatehouse inserted in it. To the west is a steep scarp, and although later landscaping has buried the rampart in some places, it reappears to the east of the North Gatehouse and runs up the steep side of the mound.

In the thirteenth century a stone curtain wall was built along the crest of the earthen rampart. The wall on the western side was largely destroyed in the nineteenth century. On the opposite side, above the town, the

Reconstruction drawing by Peter Dunn of how the buildings in the courtyard may have appeared in about 1250

wall is at its highest. There is the base of one angle of a tower midway along this eastern length, but in the south-eastern angle there is a gap caused by the collapse of the Watch (or Witches) Tower in 1830.

In the south-west corner of the courtyard is a stone-walled pit roughly square in plan, just inside the curtain wall. This is similar to the stone-lined pit in the North Gatehouse (see above) and is thought to be evidence of stone or stone-based towers supplementing the twelfth-century timber defences. Similar 'towers' also occur at Restormel Castle, further to the west near Lostwithiel.

Excavations have revealed several buildings within the courtyard. The long narrow hall opposite the ticket office and shop belongs to the thirteenth century and was built on the site of buildings constructed in the eleventh and twelfth centuries. It has an entrance on the north side. Another door in one corner led to a stone-lined latrine pit. Later this pit was filled in and a walled passage built to another pit cut into the slope of the rampart.

When excavated, the hall revealed evidence for timber benching along the walls. This, and the absence of any residential features, suggest that the hall was used for an administrative function, perhaps as a courtroom. The building went through several changes before it was demolished and the walling filled in

about 1300. Its site was occupied in the early seventeenth century by walled yards and a workshop.

A narrow 'passage' divides this building from a large square kitchen. This too was built in the thirteenth century, but had a longer life. In its later years an oven was inserted into the south wall for heating a large container, perhaps connected with brewing. Remains of a door in the north-east corner gave access into a walled yard which separated the kitchen from the Great Hall.

The Great Hall

The Great Hall also belongs to the thirteenth century and was built on the site of three predecessors. It remained in use as the Assize Hall until the early 1600s, but had been demolished and levelled by 1650. Little remains of the actual walls, since they were robbed for building material at the time of demolition: the site is marked out in the grass. The hall was of considerable size: 22m by 7m (72 x 23ft). A further building was attached on the western side. This is possibly the 'Counsell House' mentioned in 1463-65. The corner of another thirteenth-century building has been located parallel with the Great Hall.

There are other medieval buildings alongside the Victorian cottage and at the back of the South Gatehouse. The most obvious feature of these is a stone-lined latrine pit cut into the rock. It belongs to a residential block

Medieval builders constructing a tower, from a manuscript illustration of the Book of Exodus

lying underneath the cottage. This may be the site of the earl's hall and chamber, judging from the 1337 survey (see page 16). After the latrine pit had been filled in, buildings of the seventeenth century were constructed on the earlier walls, with a room added over a flight of steps giving access to the first floor of the gatehouse and the wall walk.

The cottage is a survival of the landscaping and gardening of the 1840s and 1850s. Between it and the mound, marked by the pump bearing the date 1796, is the site of the county jail, which was here until 1840.

MOUND AND HIGH TOWER

The mound was always the strong point and citadel of the defences. However, it did not attain its present height in a single operation. The early mound was lower and appears to have been set on the end of a rocky spur. The rock itself was probably cut to create a fairly steep slope on the sides away from the bailey.

The present shape is not entirely medieval. A thick packing of clay was added to the northern side in about 1700, perhaps to provide greater stability. During the later eighteenth century, perhaps as part of the garden works associated with Eagle House, the profile of the mound was distorted by the dumping of vast quantities of soil and clay. These in turn were altered during the Victorian period with the terraces and walls you can see today.

Approach to the mound

Today the mound itself is approached across a modern bridge over a thirteenth-century ditch, a significant part of Richard of Cornwall's improvements of the defences. This ditch separated the enlarged mound from the bailey, with both ends of the ditch closed by the line of the curtain wall. From the modern bridge you can see the backs of town houses encroaching on the line of the outer ditch, which still survives as a narrow lane known as Castle Dyke.

The modern bridge is built on the most recent of a series of medieval and seventeenth-century bridge piers and abutments. A small thirteenth-century D-shaped tower guarded the end of the bridge and also the stairway up the mound. Just three stones of the arch over the gateway survive. The tower is quite small, with one window or loop covering the bridge. It was no more than two storeys high.

Continuous with the tower was a wall retaining a small terrace to the left of the stairway. This terrace, known locally as 'Paradise', contains a stone-lined well. Otherwise its function is uncertain. Excavation has revealed that a ditch earlier than Richard of Cornwall's ran below the terrace; indeed the well was sunk against the inner side of the ditch.

Reconstruction drawing by Peter Dunn of the D-shaped tower as it may have appeared in about 1250

Richard of Cornwall's coat of arms on a floor tile from Cleeve Abbey, Somerset

This early ditch was crossed by a timber bridge at first and then by a series of causeways. Later the causeway and steps up the mound were flanked with masonry.

From the terrace it can be seen that the guard tower abuts an earlier length of side walling. The walled approach to the mound was roofed.

The keep

At the summit of the mound was the keep. The first stone keep consisted of a circular stone wall, principally used as a fighting platform at the level of the wall walk. The side walls of the stairway up the mound extended to the shell keep: the toothing can be seen on either side of the gateway. This gateway, which was protected by a portcullis, is also part of thirteenth-century alterations and was added to an earlier gateway. Inside the keep there were rooms, but the remains of a latrine recess on the west side is the only evidence of them now.

During the thirteenth century, the round High Tower was built within the circular stone wall and the intervening space roofed at wall-walk level. You can see the line of joist holes for this roof halfway up the tower. An outer, low wall round the edge of the mound was also added to give a further line of defence.

Access to the wall walk was by two staircases in the thickness of the wall.

One of these is on the left of the gateway, the other in a recess in the wall on the north side. This wall walk survives in places, although the parapet has almost all disappeared. On the west side of the keep there is a large recess. The outer face of this recess has entirely broken away and the only features remaining are the opening of a drain from the wall walk on the south side and the jambs of a window on either side of the opening. Originally the recess contained one or two latrine shafts flushed by water from the wall walk down the drain in wet weather.

The High Tower

The High Tower is built of dark-coloured shale quite unlike the rest of the stone on the mound. It leans about 1m (3ft 2ins) out of the vertical. Inside there are two rooms. The door on the west side with a pointed arch leads into a ground-floor room with no window. On the left of the door, a staircase in the thickness of the wall leads to the first-floor room and gives access to it and the wall walk above. The upper room is well lit by a large window with window seats, and has a large fireplace. There are the remains of a slightly projecting hood to the fireplace.

Although impressive, the High Tower had only limited residential uses. It seems to have been used as an observation point.

HISTORY OF THE
CASTLE AND TOWN

The Early Castle

Launceston is a site of great strategic importance. It stands on a ridge of high ground which falls sharply on the west and to the River Kensey on the north. The castle controlled the whole of the countryside between

Looking down the stairway to the mound at the D-shaped approach tower, with the well on the right

Bodmin Moor and Dartmoor and guarded the ford (and later bridge) at Polson, the main crossing point by land into Cornwall before the construction of the bridge over the River Tamar at Saltash.

The first historical reference to a castle at Launceston occurs in the Domesday survey of 1086 which refers to the 'count's castle at Dunhevet' (the former name of Launceston), but given the site's significance, it seems likely that the first castle was the result of the Norman military campaign in the South-West in 1067-68 to suppress a Saxon revolt in Exeter.

The 'count' referred to in the Domesday survey was Robert, Count of Mortain, half-brother of William the Conqueror and one of his closest supporters in the Norman invasion of England. His services were rewarded with vast estates in Cornwall, and it seems probable that he was installed there by 1076.

Although Robert's extensive estates extended through 20 counties,

An impression by Terry Ball of how the castle may have appeared in the late eleventh century. The buildings in the corner of the bailey are based on the results of excavation. The bailey may have been packed with similar buildings

his greatest strength lay in Cornwall, where he controlled some 247 manors. He established his court and administrative centre at Launceston, something which greatly influenced the character of the castle.

Little is known from documentary sources about the castle in the late eleventh and twelfth centuries. The castle passed out of the Mortain family in 1106 through forfeiture to the Crown after the failure of a rebellion by Count Robert's son against William II. In 1141 the earldom was granted to Reginald de Dunstanville, one of Henry I's numerous illegitimate children. He held it until his death in 1175 and it is reasonable to suppose that this period of stability was one of consolidation and building. The castle was granted to John by his brother, King Richard I, but reverted to the Crown again after John's rebellion in 1191. Among the few early historical references to the castle itself is the grant of a pension by King Stephen in favour of 'the chaplain celebrating in the chapel within the castle of Dunhevet'.

Archaeological evidence has provided a better picture of the castle at this time. The original fortified enclosure was a massive earth rampart revetted in the front by a wall, probably made of timber. This must have been insecure on such a sloping site, and some years later the rampart was heightened and a timber fighting platform built on its crest. Whether the mound in the north-eastern corner of the enclosure was part of the original defences is uncertain. If it was, it did not have its present height (which was increased substantially later). The circular stone keep on top of the mound probably belongs to the latter part of the twelfth century.

Other stone defences probably included the gatehouses. Nothing remains of the original gatehouse to the north, the Town Gate. The present structure belongs to the thirteenth century. Elsewhere along the line of defences a number of stone or stone-based towers were built towards the back of the rampart to strengthen the timber fighting platform. Two of these remain.

Within the defences it is clear that the courtyard was from the beginning packed with buildings. The southern area that has been excavated has revealed four rows of flimsy structures near the South Gatehouse – long, narrow timber houses, and roughly oval huts with cellar-like spaces below the floor. Below the site of the later great halls was a large timber hall built with massive square posts.

Associated with these buildings and the original defences were shards of pottery, not only early Norman types, but also 'bar-lug', a distinctive regional form used in Cornwall for two centuries before the Norman Conquest. This indicates some retention of local culture and fusion with the new fashions introduced by the Norman military aristocracy.

These flimsy buildings were replaced on the same sites by better-built stone-based houses set side by side. Some had a simple two-room plan: hall and chamber. One row fronted the roadway from the South Gatehouse and another row of at least three houses was placed behind the first. The timber hall was replaced in stone on much the same plan but, probably in the later twelfth century, was replaced by another on a north-south alignment.

Excavation has shown that the north side of the bailey was also occupied. The overall impression is of large numbers of people living and working in the castle during its earliest years and throughout the twelfth century. The pressure on space was such that even the rear slopes of the earth rampart were built over.

RICHARD OF CORNWALL

There was no Earl of Cornwall for the first quarter of the thirteenth century and royal nominees acted as constables of the castle. The granting of the earldom by King Henry III to his younger brother, Richard, marks the high point of the castle's history. Richard of Cornwall held the earldom between 1227 and 1272. He had a strong taste for building and architectural display and, as at other of his English possessions, he drastically reorganised and rebuilt Launceston.

Although there was little military threat, the castle's defences were ostentatiously renovated. A 'high tower' was inserted within the shell keep and the intervening space

RICHARD OF CORNWALL

Richard, the younger brother of King Henry III, was born in 1209 and held the earldom of Cornwall between 1227 and his death in 1272. A highly educated, if somewhat vain character, he was among the richest and most powerful men in the kingdom. He also had wider ambitions in European politics, and was elected 'King of the Romans' by the German princes in 1257 – a title second in importance to that of Holy Roman Emperor – although he was always a doubtful contender for becoming emperor. He travelled tirelessly throughout Europe on diplomatic missions, and around England between royal palaces and his own estates.

Richard valued his Cornish and Devon estates, in particular

The seal of Richard of Cornwall

because of the wealth derived from the local tin industry, and made numerous purchases and exchanges to increase his land-holdings in the South-West. He also used his wealth to display

his authority through ostentatious building projects.

Launceston was important as the administrative centre of his earldom, and both the castle and town received a thorough remodelling in the mid-thirteenth century.

The double-headed eagle, symbol of the Holy Roman Empire, was used by Richard of Cornwall after his election as 'King of the Romans', on a floor tile from Cleeve Abbey

roofed over. The walls flanking the mound were rebuilt and a small tower added to guard their foot. A high curtain wall, with towers on the town side, replaced the earlier timber defences. The North Gatehouse was rebuilt and the South Gatehouse refronted with solid drum towers. A fortified bridge or barbican spanned the ditch. Within the bailey there was also rebuilding. The tightly packed buildings in the south-west quarter were demolished and the site levelled. In their place the principal buildings of the castle, in particular the Great Hall, were laid out, more spaciously planned but still on the old alignment.

Reconstruction drawing by Terry Ball of the castle in the late twelfth century, based on archaeological excavation. The bailey may have been filled with buildings similar to those in the south-western corner

Reconstruction drawing by Terry Ball of the castle after Richard of Cornwall's rebuilding, in about 1270. Remains of most of the buildings shown can still be seen

The Castle in Decline

After Richard of Cornwall's death in 1272, his son, Edmund, moved the earldom's administration to Lostwithiel, and at the same time remodelled the nearby castle at Restormel. The reason for this shift of the earldom's centre of gravity was doubtless to be closer to the sources of tin production which increasingly provided a substantial proportion of the earl's revenue.

The move had its effect upon the castle at Launceston, even though it remained the centre for justice and manorial rights. Certain buildings went out of use and there was a period of neglect until the accession of Edward, the Black Prince, as the first Duke of Cornwall in 1337.

Nevertheless, some idea of the extent and complexity of the castle is revealed in the survey made by the Black Prince's officials in 1337: 'There is there a certain castle whose walls are ruinous. And they ought to be maintained by those holding knight's fees belonging to the honour of the same castle. And there are in the same castle a certain hall with two cellars that needs re-roofing, a sufficient kitchen attached to the said hall, a small upstairs hall called the earl's chamber, with a chamber and little chapel whose walls are of timber and plaster, and the timber thereof is almost disjointed. And two chambers above the two gates sufficiently covered with lead, one old and decayed little hall for the constable with a chamber and cellar and a small kitchen attached. There is also a chapel in good order apart from the

Launceston Castle, in an engraving by Samuel and Nathaniel Buck from 1734. The building in the centre of the courtyard is the county jail

To Sᴿ WILLIAM MORICE Barᵗ
This Prospect is most gratefully Inscribed by.

Launceston alias Dunheved Castle, was a very strong place, and there
obtain'd, the name of Castle Terrible, the round Hill on which it stan
being environ'd with a triple wall. It was built by William de Mort
Earl of Cornwall, soon after the Conquest; & was one of the Principal

windows which are decayed, two stables for 10 horses in good order, a jail badly and inadequately covered with lead and another prison called "the larder" weak and almost useless. And one passage leading from the castle up to the high tower newly covered with lead but the steps of which are defective. And there are in the same tower two chambers whose doors and windows are of no value. And the aforesaid tower has two mantlet walls of stone of which one portion containing by estimation three perches had fallen to the ground.'

A number of the structures described in this survey can be identified today. The hall with two cellars (i.e. a first-floor hall) has been identified by excavation and the kitchen attached to it is now exposed and visible. The earl's chamber may be the residential building known to lie underneath the Victorian cottage. The window to the chamber in the South Gatehouse can be seen, while the accommodation for the constable existed in the North Gatehouse until the eighteenth century and its 'cellar' (ground-floor room) can still be seen. The features of the High Tower are also clearly visible. The exact sites of the chapel, stables and jails have yet to be identified.

Repairs were started in 1341. The Great Hall was repaired and re-roofed, as was the South Gatehouse. Twelve years later

the Black Prince (now Duke of Cornwall) and his council met at Launceston Castle. Accounts of various repairs to the castle continue to appear throughout the fifteenth century.

Buildings such as 'Rekilly Chamber', the 'Queen's Hall', the 'Justice's Chamber', the 'Council Chamber next the Great Hall' are recorded, and it seems that the bailey was divided into two by a long wall between the chapel and the North Gate.

The needs of justice required the continuing existence of the castle, and in particular its Great Hall and the various jails. By the time of John Leland's visit in 1539, he mentions the chapel and 'hall for assizes and sessions' but does not comment on the rest of the castle. The hall continued in use until the end of Elizabeth's reign – it was described as very spacious in 1584 – but by 1650 both it and the chapel had been completely levelled.

Civil War

During the Civil War the town and castle were held for the king, except for two occasions in 1642 and 1644 when they were occupied by the Parliamentarians before they were finally captured by Fairfax's army on 25 February 1646. There was then an attempt to patch up the defences. An entry in the town records for April 1646 refers to '4 days work' on making up the castle wall and other work on the town wall. However, the survey of 1650 indicated that by then the only part of the castle remaining habitable was the North Gatehouse containing the two rooms in which the constable lived. Houses and gardens occupied the ditch separating the castle from the town. The extent of the general decay of the castle and the disappearance of the internal buildings is strongly emphasised by the fact that it was not deemed necessary to apply the usual Parliamentarian policy of 'slighting', or dismantling a castle's buildings.

History of the Town

Robert of Mortain established the town of Launceston at about the same time as the castle by transferring an existing market from the control of the canons of St Stephen's, a mile away to the north, to the new castle. In time, a corruption of the name, Lan Stefan, was assumed by Dunhevet (the original name of the castle). The town gradually developed under the shadow of the castle, deriving much of its importance from the administrative functions connected with the castle as the centre of the earldom.

Outside the town, by the crossing of the River Kensey, the canons of St Stephen's were refounded as an Augustinian priory in 1127. Remains of the priory can be seen today by St Thomas's church. In the mid-thirteenth century, as part of his reconstruction of the castle, Richard of Cornwall added a stone wall around the town, with three gateways, of which only one survives today. Launceston was the only walled town in Cornwall.

The priory was dissolved in 1536, but the parish church of St Mary Magdalen had been expensively rebuilt only a few years earlier by Sir Henry Trecarrel. The town itself prospered throughout the sixteenth to eighteenth centuries from its connection with the assizes and its role as the county town, in addition to being a thriving market town for the local area. The many surviving houses of this period in streets such as Castle Street display how prosperous the town was at this time.

By the nineteenth century, however, other towns were starting to grow at Launceston's expense as they benefited more from the impact of the Industrial Revolution in Cornwall and Devon. Launceston was also seen as inconvenient as the county town, lying near the border with Devon, rather than more centrally in the county like Bodmin or Truro. In the Great Reform Act of 1832, Launceston (and Newport, its 'suburb' at the crossing over the River Kensey) lost their right to elect four MPs to Parliament, while in 1838 the assizes and the seat of county government were moved to Bodmin.

*Oil painting of Launceston
by Hendrick Frans de Cort
(1742-1810), showing
a view of the castle from
St Catherine's Hill*

LATER HISTORY OF THE CASTLE

The main prison was in the castle courtyard, and was bought from the constable by the county for use as the county jail. Various contemporary drawings show that it lay between the present Victorian cottage and the outer mound ditch. It was a relatively small building: there were three cells for female prisoners and four cells and a day room for men, plus an apartment for the governor on the first floor. A visit by the prison reformer John Howard in 1779 revealed its cramped and squalid conditions.

Elsewhere in the castle there were various smallholdings and pigsties. Irregular burials, presumably of former prisoners, were found within the castle bailey in the late nineteenth century and in the course of more recent excavations. Hangings took place in the bailey, with the last execution said to have taken place in 1821.

A major change in the condition of the castle occurred in 1764 when the constable's lodgings above the North Gatehouse were demolished. A former mayor, Coryndon Carpenter, won a lottery and from the proceeds built Eagle House, an impressive brick-fronted mansion, immediately outside the North Gate, using the gatehouse for building materials. A great deal of landscaping was done at the same time, and the curtain wall between the gatehouse and the

FAMOUS PRISONERS

The North Gatehouse, while continuing to be the traditional lodgings of the constable (an honorary post that came to be included among

George Fox and fellow Quakers in Doomsdale: an engraving by Robert Spence (1870–1964) for an edition of Fox's 'Journal'

the perquisites of the town's mayor), was also a prison.

One of its more celebrated prisoners was George Fox, founder of the Society of Friends or 'Quakers'. Fox was arrested in 1656 for distributing religious pamphlets in the town. He refused to remove his hat when brought before the magistrate, whereupon he was imprisoned for several months. He called the 'pit' into which he was put 'Doomsdale', and recorded it in his *Journal* as 'a nasty stinking place . . . all like mire, in some places to the top of our shoes in water'.

Another earlier prisoner was the Catholic priest Cuthbert Mayne, who was imprisoned in the castle, tried at the assizes and executed at Launceston in November 1577. Mayne was

Cuthbert Mayne, from a seventeenth-century print

the first Roman Catholic priest sent into England to be executed during Elizabeth I's reign, and had been sheltering in the household of a member of the local gentry, Sir Francis Tregain, before being captured by the authorities. He was canonised by Pope Paul VI in 1970.

mound was demolished or buried. The jail itself was demolished in 1842 after the assizes had moved to Bodmin. This removed the last vestige of the castle's medieval functions. The Duke of Northumberland, who had a house nearby at Werrington Park, had the castle turned into a public park and garden. This landscaping did nothing to preserve the remains of the

castle. Huts from a hospital built for the US Army during the 1940s in the courtyard further disfigured the castle's site. In 1951 the castle, which had been leased to the Corporation of Launceston by the Duchy of Cornwall, was transferred into the guardianship of the then Ministry of Works. Since 1984 the castle has been in the care of English Heritage.